Programming Concepts for the Non-Programmer

L. Christopher Bird

Introduction:

This guide has a few different origins. The text from which this edition is derived from is a series of notecards that I wrote under the name ZenMondo Wormser to teach the art of scripting in the Virtual World of Second Life. There were two sections, one teaching concepts that underly nearly any programing language, and a second section that presented a primer for Linden Scripting Language (LSL), the scripting language used in Second Life.

The lessons themselves I learned from my Father, Lonnie Bleu Bird who himself was a programmer who began his career in the 1970s. When I was young, he gave me a flow-chart template and convinced me it was a toy and taught me many concepts such as logical program flow, and how to count in binary as rules-based games.

The main task I use for the examples and lessons in this book are derived from one of these childhood games.

To be a successful programmer, you will need some basic programming skills. The skills are as follows:

> A. Logic: Breaking a task into logical steps
>
> B: Functions: When you want to do the same logical steps at different points in your program.
>
> C: Loops: doing a set of logical steps over and over.
>
> D: Conditionals: Also known as If Then Else statements.
>
> E: Functions Revisited, Passing and Returning.

These concepts are universal to many programming languages, but how they are implemented in each language may be quite different. I do not use any actual programming language in this book, but it is structurally similar to LSL, which in itself is similar to the c programming language, and languages derived from c.

It is my hypothesis that learning the underlying concepts will serve one better than learning how to accomplish tasks procedurally, and it with that in mind that the instruction is geared.

This is not a passive book, there will be exercises, and following them, a guide to evaluating how you did.   So, without further ado, let us begin!

– L. Christopher Bird

Programming Concepts: Logic

Logic is the main tool in any programmer's toolbox. All programs begin and end with their logic -- the breaking down of a program into its logical steps. It is said that once you have the **LOGIC** of a program, the difficult part is done, then its just a matter of coding it.

To Begin Thinking Logically let's take a real-world task and break it down to its logical steps. Let's make a sandwich. Use the space below to record your steps for making a peanut butter & jelly sandwich. Yes, I am asking you to write in this book. Use the rest of the page if you want to.

How I Make a Peanut Butter & Jelly Sandwich

Actually, go ahead and use this page too...

Now that you have done that, let us compare it to this sample:

How to Make a Peanut Butter & Jelly Sandwich

Plant Wheat.
Grow Wheat.
Harvest Wheat.
Grind Wheat and make flour.
Add Water and Yeast to the flour.
Bake dough, make bread.

Plant Strawberries.
Grow Strawberries.
Harvest Strawberries.
Mash Strawberries.
Boil mashed strawberries with sugar.
Add Pectin.
Let set, make jelly.

Plant Peanuts.
Grow Peanuts.
Harvest Peanuts.
Grind Peanuts, make Peanut Butter.

Slice Bread.
Take Two Slices of Bread, lay flat.
Find Knife.
Use Knife to spread peanut butter on one piece of bread.
Use Knife to spread Jelly on other piece of bread.
Clean Knife.
Find Plate.
Place Pieces of bread together, Peanut Butter & Jelly to the inside.
Place sandwich on plate.

A little more detail than you were expecting? Sometimes in programming we have to take a task and break it into very tiny parts. Things we would think of that come naturally or are "common sense" do not necessarily come naturally to a computer program.

EVERYTHING MUST BE SPELLED OUT.

Programming Concepts: Functions

Functions are a collection of logical steps that one would want to re-use or do more than once in a program. Functions can also be handy for organizing your code into manageable chunks. Say we had to write instructions for making two Peanut Butter & Jelly sandwiches to someone that could only handle one task at a time. We could simply state the instructions twice, or define a function once, and call it twice.

So first we would write the function for making a sandwich like so:

```
MakeSandwich ()
{
    Plant Wheat.
    Grow Wheat.
    Harvest Wheat.
    Grind Wheat and make flour.
    Add Water and Yeast to the flour.
    Bake dough, make bread.

    Plant Strawberries.
    Grow Strawberries.
    Harvest Strawberries.
    Mash Strawberries.
    Boil mashed strawberries with sugar.
    Add Pectin.
    Let set make jelly.

    Plant Peanuts.
    Grow Peanuts.
    Harvest Peanuts.
    Grind Peanuts, make Peanut Butter.

    Slice Bread.
    Take Two Slices of Bread, lay flat.
    Find Knife.
    Use Knife to spread peanut butter on one piece of bread.
    Use Knife to spread Jelly on other piece of bread.
    Clean Knife.
    Find Plate.
    Place Pieces of bread together, Peanut Butter & Jelly to   the inside.
```

        Place sandwich on plate.
}

So now our program to make two sandwiches will be fairly simple, just two lines:

```
MakeSandwich();
MakeSandwich();
```

Each time we say "MakeSandwich();" what we really are doing is using a label to execute all the instructions defined by the function declaration.

But here I have broken one of the cardinal rules of a good function:

A GOOD FUNCTION SHOULD ONLY DO ONE THING.

In this version of MakeSandwich() we are also making bread, jelly, and peanut butter. Let's break it into 4 functions: MakeBread(), MakeJelly(), MakePeanutButter(), and MakeSandwich().

Time to write in the book again!

Write your four sandwich making functions here:

```
MakeBread()
{
        //Put your instructions here between the braces




}

MakeJelly()
{
        //Put your instructions here between the braces
```

```
}
MakePeanutButter()
{
        //Put your instructions here between the braces




}

MakeSandwich()
{
 //Put your instructions here between the braces







}
```

Now that you have done that, compare it to this example:

```
MakeBread()
{
  Plant Wheat.
  Grow Wheat.
  Harvest Wheat.
  Grind Wheat and make flour.
  Add Water and Yeast to the flour.
  Bake dough, make bread.
}

MakeJelly()
{
  Plant Strawberries.
```

```
      Grow Strawberries.
      Harvest Strawberries.
      Mash Strawberries.
      Boil mashed strawberries with sugar.
      Add Pectin.
      Let set make jelly.
}

MakePeanutButter()
{
   Plant Peanuts.
   Grow Peanuts.
   Harvest Peanuts.
   Grind Peanuts, make Peanut Butter.
}

MakeSandwich()
{
   Slice Bread.
   Take Two Slices of Bread, lay flat.
   Find Knife.
   Use Knife to spread peanut butter on one piece of bread.
   Use Knife to spread Jelly on other piece of bread.
   Clean Knife.
   Find Plate.
   Place Pieces of bread together, Peanut Butter & Jelly to the inside.
   Place sandwich on plate.
}
```

Now our program will be a bit longer, but the functions make for cleaner code.

```
MakeBread();
MakeJelly();
MakePeanutButter();
MakeSandwich();

MakeBread();
MakeJelly();
MakePeanutButter();
MakeSandwich();
```

But even this can be improved. Since we need to call the functions MakeBread(), MakeJelly(), and MakePeanutButter() (let us pretend these functions only make enough for one sandwich) each time we call the function MakeSandwich(), we should put those functions INSIDE the MakeSandwich() function.

YOU CAN CALL FUNCTIONS FROM WITHIN FUNCTIONS.

So the New MakeSandwich() function should now look like this:

```
MakeSandwich()
{
  MakeBread();
  MakeJelly();
  MakePeanutButter();

  Slice Bread.
  Take Two Slices of Bread, lay flat.
  Find Knife.
  Use Knife to spread peanut butter on one piece of bread.
  Use Knife to spread Jelly on other piece of bread.
  Clean Knife.
  Find Plate.
  Place Pieces of bread together, Peanut Butter & Jelly to the inside.
  Place sandwich on plate.
}
```

So now our program to make two peanut butter & jelly sandwiches looks like this:

```
MakeSandwich();
MakeSandwich();
```

If we wanted to make 3 Sandwiches, we just add another line. If we wanted to make 10, we would just call MakeSandwich() 10 times. But that is inefficient. What we want to use is a **loop**. This will be covered in the next lesson.

Programming Concepts: Loops

When a repetitive task needs to be done, an efficient way to code this is a *loop*. A loop will continue until its break condition is met.

Let's say we wanted to make 10 sandwiches

```
while(there are less than 10 sandwiches)
{
   MakeSandwich();
}
```

This looks pretty good, but it will not work quite right. This is what is called an **Infinite Loop**. Why? Because the break condition is never met.

Wait a minute you say, "the loop will make 10 sandwiches", yes it will, but the loop doesn't know how many sandwiches it has made. **You must provide a count**, it cannot count on its own.

```
while(sandwich_count is less than 10)
{
   MakeSandwich();
   Add 1 to sandwich_count;
}
```

So, this is how the loop works. First it evaluates the condition inside the parenthesis. (sandwich count is less than 10). If it is *TRUE,* then the instructions between the braces:

```
{
   MakeSandwich();
   Add 1 to sandwich_count;
}
```

are executed. **All** of the instructions are executed. Once they are done, the condition inside the parenthesis is evaluated again. If it is TRUE, the loop executes again. If the condition is evaluated as FALSE (that is, sandwich count is NOT less than 10) then the loop breaks, and the code inside the braces is not executed.

Let's say we have two functions. MakePeanutButterAndJellySandwich() and MakeBolognaSandwich(). and one variable sandwich_count. Using these we want to make 5 Peanut Butter and Jelly Sandwiches, and 15 Bologna Sandwiches. Write your program in the space below.

My Sandwich Making Program with Loops

I have generously given you more blank paper to continue writing your program:

Now that you have done that, compare it to this example:

```
//Example Sandwich Making Program with Loops
// Will make 5 peanut butter & Jelly sandwiches
// and make 15 bologna sandwiches.

Make sandwich_count equal 0;

while(sandwich_count is less than 5)
{
    MakePeanutButterAndJellySandwich();
    Add 1 to sandwich_count;
}

Make sandwich_count equal 0;

while(sandwich_count is less than 15)
{
    MakeBolognaSandwich();
    Add 1 to sandwich_count;
}
```

Notice two things:

1) The code for each loop is the same size, even though we are making different amounts of sandwiches.

2) the line:
    Make sandwich_count equal 0;

This is called **initializing your counter**. It is important to *INTIALIZE YOUR COUNTER BEFORE ENTERING A LOOP.*

Let's look at what would happen if you did not initialize your counter.

We will assume that the uninitialized value of sandwich_count is 0, but we cannot rely on this.
First, we make 5 sandwiches

```
while(sandwich_count is less than 5)
{
```

```
    MakePeanutButterAndJellySandwich();
    Add 1 to sandwich_count;
}
```

Right now, the sandwich counter is 5. Then we enter into the second loop.

```
while(sandwich_count is less than 15)
{
    MakeBolognaSandwich();
    Add 1 to sandwich_count;
}
```

We continue to use sandwich_count which is already at five. After the first time through the loop it will be at 6, until it arrives at 15 and meets the break condition and exits. But in the end, we will only have 10 Bologna Sandwiches.

Another way you could have done the second loop without re-initializing the counter is to make the break condition be:

```
while(sandwich_count is less than 20)
```

This would work but would make the code less clear to read. Sometimes it is worth taking an extra step to make your code more readable, which in the long term, make it easier to maintain if you (or someone else) needs to modify at a later time (sometimes much later).

Programming Concepts: Conditionals

Sometimes a computer program needs to make a decision. How it makes this decision is it is asked a Yes or No question, and does a certain thing based on the answer.

Let's say we have a sandwich making robot which can make either peanut butter & jelly sandwiches, or make bologna sandwiches. It needs a program to take an order to know what kind of sandwich to make.

Now a computer can only answer **YES OR NO** questions. So, we can't simply ask, "what kind of sandwich do you want?" We must be more specific. We must ask "Do you want a peanut butter & jelly sandwich?" which can be answered yes or no. **IF** the answer is yes, **THEN** we can do one thing, **ELSE** if the answer is no, we can do another. This is called an **IF THEN ELSE** structure or sometimes just called **IF-ELSE**

Consider the following program.

```
Ask "Do you Want a Peanut Butter and Jelly Sandwich?

Get Answer

IF(Answer is YES)
{
    MakePeanutButterJellySandwich();  //This is a function
}

ELSE  //This means the answer was NOT Yes
{
    MakeBolognaSandwich();
}
```

Now looking at this program, it will only make one kind of sandwich at a time. **IF** the answer is **YES**, it will Make a Peanut Butter and Jelly Sandwich and not make a Bologna Sandwich. If the answer in **NOT YES** it jumps over the part of the code that makes a Peanut Butter & Jelly Sandwich and executes the code to make a Bologna Sandwich. This is called a **CONDITIONAL JUMP**.

Notice that the program is only looking for an answer of "YES". This program would not know the difference between the word "No" or "Sasquatch". Either of those answers would result in the sandwich-making robot making a bologna sandwich. Also, it only looks for the answer, "Yes" so answers of "Yeah", "Y", and "Yes, I would like that very much, sandwich-bot." would also result in the robot making a bologna sandwich. Our hypothetical sandwich making robot is not very smart, but what do you expect with only six lines of code?

Programming Concepts: Functions, Revisited

In a previous lesson we learned a function can be a handy way to reuse some code that we want to use more than once. But functions have another trick, *passing* and *returning* data.

One can think of passing as giving the function something to work with and returning is what the function gives back to when called. Another way to look at this is, a function is *PASSED* (given) input and *RETURNS* (gives) output.

Let's say we have function that can make either a Peanut Butter & Jelly sandwich, or a Bologna sandwich. It will decide what to make based on what is passed to the function, and return the sandwich asked for. It may look something like this:

What is returned by the function is defined to the left of the function name and what is passed to the function is put in the parenthesis.

```
sandwich MakeSandwich(sandwich_type)
{
   IF(sandwich_type is "Peanut Butter and Jelly")
   {
      RETURN MakePeanutButerJellySanwich();
   }

   IF(sandwich_type is "Bologna")
   {
      RETURN MakeBolognaSandwich();
   }
```

```
    ELSE
    {
      RETURN "I don't know how to make that kind of sandwich";
    }
}
```

Now we are assuming that MakePeanutButterJellySandwich() and MakeBolognaSandwich() also return the sandwich they made which is then returned by MakeSandwich. Functions can be chained this way. Now an example of using the function in a program.

```
my_sandwich = MakeSandwich("Peanut Butter and Jelly");  //Will get a PB& J Sandwich
my_sandwich2 = MakeSandwich("Bologna"); //Will get a bologna sandwich
my_sandwich3 = MakeSandwich("Cucumber"); //Will have no sandwich and the error message.
```

We store what the function returns to the left of calling the function and using an equal sign and pass the function its data in the parenthesis.

Programming Concepts: Go forth, and code.

That's it.

If you have understood the preceding, you are absolutely ready to tackle the programming language of your choice. Now the particulars of the language(s) you choose will have their own ways of going about things, and the particulars of the platform(s) you are coding for will have their own challenges to them. But these four concepts are universal to computer programming. These concepts are a foundation, a foundation that can be used time and time again for programming tasks. But a foundation is only at the bottom; it is up to **YOU** to build upon it.

Dedication

To my father who convinced me a flow-chart template was a toy, and that a line of pennies were in fact, a machine that operated by rules.

To Ada Lovelace, Queen of Engines, and Queen of my Heart. She blazed the trail that every programmer after her has followed since 1842, when she invented the concepts explained in this book. Alas, history has not recorded if she liked sandwiches.

- LCB, Modesto, California

www.ingramcontent.com/pod-product-compliance
Lightning Source LLC
Chambersburg PA
CBHW080606060326
40689CB00021B/4949